Navigating the Dysfunctions of Nonprofit Management

Staying Afloat Without A Life Jacket

Tonya R. Bryan

ISBN-10: 1548422282

ISBN-13: 978-1548422288

TABLE OF CONTENTS

PREFACE

This is not a book about any specific agency for which I've worked as an employee or consultant. It is a culmination of my experiences and insight gained while working within the nonprofit culture.

I was led to write this book because many nonprofit leaders are having similar experiences and need to know that they are not alone in the struggle.

Within the contents of this book I share my most complex experiences in navigating within a dysfunctional system.

Interestingly, that while writing, there were no two situations that mirrored one another. For me, this notes the depth and breadth of the dysfunction and supports my argument of the challenges and skills needed in order to navigate within this culture.

Although my experiences are not limited to social services, my view is primarily based on the social service sector. I've learned that the "cookie cutter" model of nonprofit is more prevalent in national models.

The thought from which I drew the subtitle, "Staying Afloat without a Life Jacket", speaks to the many times I felt as though I was drowning and managed to stay afloat. There have been times when I've needed support and was left to figure it out on my own.

I succeeded because of my curiosity for learning and attaining knowledge that would aid in my survival and success. I recommend that as you read this book you process what is written, reflect on its contents and be encouraged.

ACKNOWLEDGMENTS

To my Son and Mother who waited patiently for me to get home from work after working twelve to fourteen hours and even bringing work home to complete; Thank you for your love and support. I love you both immensely.

To everyone serving in the Nonprofit sector and is navigating the dysfunctions within nonprofit management, continue to serve with a heart of compassion and faithfulness to the mission of the work.

Thank you to those who have impacted my life and taught me the "do's and don'ts" of nonprofit leadership that shaped me into the leader I am today.

To every barrier that I have had to cross in order to reach this place in my life, I thank you for being there, for you have taught me to endure and have given me the persistence I needed to survive.

To Rev. Dr. Renita Weems who challenged the Princeton Theological Seminary Black Theology and Leadership Institute (PTSBTLI) '16 Fellows to leave a body of work for the next generation. This is my first contribution.

To my editors, Tonya McCombs and Tanisha Eileen Tuck, THANK YOU, THANK YOU, THANK YOU!!! There are no adequate words to express my gratitude for all that you've done.

INTRODUCTION

So often books are written to talk about how to overcome obstacles, change systems or new strategies to improve leadership and/or service delivery. However, we never talk about the dysfunctions that lead to these obstacles and how we navigate this culture within organizations.

Nonprofit organizations are not cookie-cutter models. Social Service nonprofit organizations, I believe, have the most challenges in terms of service delivery and day-to-day operations.

You will not find many citations from other experts in the field of nonprofit management within the contents of this body of work.   I am writing from experience; a place of success, joy and pain. Many nonprofit executives live a silent career of functioning within a dysfunctional system that is only spoken about amongst those whom they can trust. Some will work with you as long as it serves their purpose. Some will work with you for your connections and access to resources. Often times,

those same people will ostracize you and become allies with those who are working against you for their own selfish gain.

I have been privileged to serve several community-based nonprofit organizations with a large presence and strong history within their perspective communities. I have also served a nonprofit organization with a National brand; a statewide nonprofit and local government. Each of these organizations, including the local government, continue to do amazing and impactful work towards the common good of addressing poverty, strengthening families, providing mentors, community engagement, etc.

It is my hope that as you turn the pages of this book, you will find a familiar scenario of which you can relate. I hope as you continue to read you are able to breathe a sigh of relief knowing that someone else has had the same experiences. I have stepped out and called a "thing" a "thing" and yes It Is dysfunctional.

The intent of this work is not to demean the service provided by anyone or any agency in particular, but to merely shed light on a world that is seldom talked about publicly.   This is the time and season for nonprofit leaders to understand that they are not alone in this culture of functioning within a dysfunctional system that continues to perpetuate itself.   Due to the lack of courage and the culture of this secret society it retards your intellect and dulls your shine.

Know that even in this space, you are walking in your purpose and called to be a change agent regardless of the waves crashing all around you.   You will stay afloat...I did.

A LOOK INSIDE

For all intents and purposes, the contents of this work are based on my 20+ years experience in nonprofit organizations. I have had a wonderful career serving people within the community from all walks of life. I have seen the breakdown of people who come for assistance when the bottom had fallen out. I have witnessed emotional breakdowns as a result of hunger pangs where a person could not clearly articulate their needs for coming for assistance due to the urgency of immediate need for food. I have also witnessed homeless people with unaddressed mental illnesses; unable to control their behaviors where they're posing a threat to everyone within their immediate space and to those working to service their immediate needs.   I have had to close locations due to active gunfire within close proximity of the program site.

I've had to make decisions to close the office early due to the lack of heat and/or air conditioning, depending on the season. Decisions had to be made whether you close, delay opening or have an early dismissal during snow storms. Whatever your decision, be prepared that a board member may not agree with your decision, even though you have made the decision based on the possible attendance and staff safety.

I've been on both sides of the delayed payroll saga. I've been the Executive who has had to inform staff of a payroll delay and I've been in the position of the staffer receiving the message of a delayed pay. I've even worked for six weeks without pay waiting for the national organization to come to our aid. In fact, this is not as uncommon as many would believe. It remains unspoken and is part of navigating the dysfunctions of nonprofit management.

I've witnessed a colleague's car get totaled after being hit by a stolen car that crashed into their vehicle in front of the workplace. I've been told not to go outside because there was a shoot out outside of the agency.

In other instances, when providing youth services, some youth have stolen from the very people tasked with assisting them. You provide food referrals to consumers who steal items from the office. I remember a client who stole an entire case of water and returned to the office the next day for assistance. When he returned we confronted him about stealing the water. Of course he denied it and we proceeded to provide him with the aid he needed.

I've experienced being in a location alone and a prostitute, hiding from the police, enters the office pretending to seek job search assistance and you find yourself speaking to her and letting her know that she has a greater purpose in life. As she begins to cry she opens up and tells you that she was a registered nurse before her life was turned upside down by a drug dependency. There have been people who have not met the requirements for assistance and have asked me what they were going to do and I had no answer for them.

These are just a few examples of the work we are tasked with in the nonprofit Social Service sector. In the midst of it all, we must continue to meet the needs and adhere to the guidelines of our funders. We must answer to a board that may not fully understand the breadth and depth of the day-to-day function of the particular organization.

As with any family or those within whom you are in close relation, there are personality conflicts. These conflicts can be mean spirited and actually cruel, especially when written anonymously to the Administrator, Board and even funders. Some of these correspondence had been received through fictitious email addresses, through snail mail and left under the office door. Because you have never experienced anything like this in your career you find these actions and behaviors unconscionable. My experience has been if I find myself unhappy with my job, leadership and the direction of my career, I merely seek another opportunity. I would never think of writing mean letters in an attempt to jeopardize someone else's employment. I would never have thought to go to the Equal Employment Opportunity Commission and file a false complaint in an attempt to cause someone to lose their job. Yes, this is all true. These accounts are my personal experiences that will be discussed, in detail, in a later chapter. Yet, I continued to press forward and tended to the matters at hand.

Do these actions hit you in the gut and knock the wind out of you for a second? Absolutely! Then you realize your purpose is to serve the community and move the mission. This may not be your story but I'm sure there is some area in which you can identify. Every nonprofit organization is not a "cookie cutter" model and comes with its own ups and downs. However, the role of the administrator and its challenges remain the same. There are not enough hours in the day, month or year to complete every task at hand. In fact, you need to replicate yourself at least six times in order to get all of the work done and be able to take a vacation.

As the administrator, your role can transition from Executive, to front line staff, to food preparer and server, to front desk receptionist all while writing proposals, tending to staff needs, putting out every fire that is visible and tending to the smoldering piles of debris set by staff. This is what I call functioning in the dysfunction and navigating your way within the culture. If you are not committed to the cause of the mission, you will have great difficulty staying afloat.

I remember one day, in the afternoon the Executive Director came to our location and terminated both my supervisor and the Department Director. Everyone was in shock and didn't know what to do or how to react. I was told that I would now oversee the department. Having little knowledge of some of the programs I became a quick learner and ultimately mastered the two programs I knew little about. I had to read the contracts and not only understand the services we were contracted to perform but I also had to learn the language of these two new programs which differed vastly. One was healthcare and the other was an afterschool program. I learned what I needed in order to successfully operate both programs and learned a great deal during that time.

Along the way I met great people who would provide guidance and support to ensure my continued success. It was also during this time that I became an instant supervisor. I now had a staff and had to navigate within this role as well. Again, with the help of mentors who supported me and a wonderful staff, this transition was not difficult.

As a result, of this experience, I implemented the process of having newly hired supervisors, managers and directors read the programmatic portion of their contract in order to fully understand the expectations and outcomes of their specified program. This is not common because often times within this culture of dysfunction, directors do not want to divulge this information to staff. However, this is the best way for nonprofit leaders to be trained and also understand the undertaking of their role. For me, the most growth I've had in any position was when I was given information to read. This makes the first week more productive and gives opportunity to ask specific questions regarding the program. There is more to a role than what is outlined in a job description. Initial intense training is paramount to any level of success within the nonprofit culture.

I've often thought my situation was limited to me and my agency until I began speaking with other colleagues who had become friends. One day as I sat amongst very knowledgeable individuals who were well versed in nonprofit culture, as well as teachers in academia, and spoke about navigating these dysfunctions. Someone at the table made a statement that emancipated me from my thinking about this crazed culture of nonprofit. He stated that even when the smartest and most successful business person enters into the nonprofit arena, after the first Board meeting they lose something. This individual had observed this firsthand and truly understood the culture. He understood how the confidence of some Executive Director's becomes shattered by the lack of support or barraging of a Board of Directors or the lack of support from the Board. These community and faith based leaders and educators understood the challenges of having to accomplish much with a staff that possesses limited skills. These leaders understood the many challenges of funding that cause mission creep, which is slowly veering away from your organizations purpose.

The Board directs leaders to "get money" and the leaders begin to add programs and services that are outside of their mission. These leaders understood the culture of chasing the grant money and adding services in order to increase funds to meet the annual organizational budget. This pressure is a major cause of organizations straying away from their actual mission and scope of services. For example, the mission of your organization is to provide mentoring services for youth. Due to cuts in current funding, leaders begin to discover funding opportunities for families. They rationalize their submission of an application because, after all, you are providing services to children who are a part of a family. Makes perfect sense, you tell yourself. Wrong! It was just that easy to creep away from your mission of mentoring youth.

After the conversation over our meal I thought, Alas, there was someone who understood the plight of the nonprofit leader and was not afraid to speak it.

In order to stay afloat, you must surround yourself with a group of people who will guide you and support you when you are right and when you are wrong or not in a positive state of mind. These individuals will bring you back to your reality.

Nonprofit leadership is lonely because you cannot trust everyone and must understand that everyone does not have your best interest at heart. As a nonprofit leader you must be able to set boundaries and never cross them. Although you may have full trust and confidence in your staff and full board support, you must remember the relationship, no matter how friendly, must remain professional. Otherwise, you may be setting yourself up for false accusations such as favoritism and allegations of hiring friends.   I must say that I love and respect my friends too much to bring them into a culture where I am treated less than they feel I deserve.

I was told by a mentor that I must decide if I could out serve the board chairperson who may not be in agreement with my leadership.   Can you out last the tenure of your board chairperson? What if there are no tenures, then what?   There have been skilled Executives who have been able to transition their entire Board out and bring in new members with fresh ideas who are willing to work towards the success and sustainability of the organization. However, this is not the norm but it can be done.

Working within this culture is a balancing act and needs precise navigation skills.

"Functioning in the dysfunction is working with an ever revolving door of individuals due to the organizations inability to provide competitive salaries, flexible hours and compensation packages in a very stressful environment."

ROLE PLAY

As an administrator, you must be married to the cause and mission of the work. You must understand that nonprofits, whether community or faith based, are not a "one size fits all" model. There are cultural differences within each organization.

If your work is geared towards education, you may experience challenges differing from that of a social service mission. If you are a social service organization your work will differ from an organization that trains leaders or one whose purpose is to develop affordable housing. Perhaps your organization is youth driven and you tend to the needs of not only youth but their families as well. All of these organizations have varying missions and stakeholders. The makeup of your team will differ based on the needs of your community and its constituents. You may be staffed with teachers, social workers (both licensed and clinical), community planners, and/or those with expertise that will equip your team to carry out the work of the mission. If you provide drug and alcohol counseling, your staff would, or should include someone who is certified to provide this service.

The nonprofit dysfunction comes when we place the wrong people in critical positions due to their longevity with the organization and we allow their passion to usurp their experiences and credentials. In doing this, we do our organizations and its consumers a disservice. We move the secretary from her role due to the loss of funding and they now become a case manager. We move the maintenance person to the front desk because they are cordial and have proven to be a team player. Again, we are doing our work and consumers a disservice.

There are performance standards for these roles. For example, if the team player has the proper background and education, and for whatever reason they settled for a lesser position out of desperation for employment. This happens, but should not be a best practice that we ascribe to. I know, I know...you had to layoff the nice lady in the accounting department and because she has been so helpful and with the agency for such a long time, you moved her into the role of a case manager. After all, she is dedicated to the organization.

****

We lose funding and have to reorganize our team. As a result, team members may or will perform two job functions without complaining. Are you making them feel appreciated or is your attitude as an administrator one that feels they should be happy to have a job? Never assume someone is happy in a role that has been "put" upon them without being given an option to decline.

What roles are indispensable and how can you effectively restructure your organization? This is the challenge nonprofit administrators and managers are met with on a regular basis. It is indeed a challenge to articulate these changes to a Board of Directors who seem to have more of an interest in governing the administrator than learning about the day-to-day functions of the organization. Without the Board of Directors or Trustees understanding the actual work of the agency they are unable to guide effectively. They may have approved the mission but may not have fully bought into the agency's mission. Therefore, they lack understanding of the many nuances faced with general operations, funding and the overall culture of the organization. There may be members who do not agree with the mission but serve to build their resume or to open other doors for other opportunities for their self-promotion. "Functioning in Dysfunction".

Team members stay at organizations because they are happy, feel appreciated and have grown in their career. Nowadays, those entering into the workforce are not looking to retire at an organization. They are looking for a first experience, a place to learn so they can gather the skills and experience needed to take them to the next plateau in their career. It's not personal...it's business.

Functioning in the dysfunction is working with an ever revolving door of individuals due to the organizations inability to provide competitive salaries, flexible hours and compensation packages in a very stressful environment.

How can we retain talent and assure we are doing everything we can to consistently develop our team? Although it's a challenge to coordinate, it is imperative that you plan quarterly staff development days. There is no need to look at the latest trends on staff development. You must be able to identify the needs of your team and plan accordingly. I've planned everything from yoga, color prism, full day training discussing best practices, full day potluck lunch training session, customer service and staff presentations to educate and inform staff of all program services provided.

What is also needed within the social service nonprofit is a "clinical supervision" component for those who provide case management. Although they do not hold the title of a Social Worker, their role consists of listening to the issues, concerns and needs of consumers all day everyday. They maintain copious case files that include data collection, analysis, plans, referrals, goals, contact logs, follow-up, etc. Without the clinical component or a professional with whom they can release some of their stress, the release manifests towards the other team members where I have witnessed a team member exhibit the personality and behaviors of the client/consumer. Therefore, it is extremely important that there be weekly time built into the work schedule for case managers to decompress all the emotions they have experienced while working with their clients. With this opportunity, stress and burnout would be minimized.

As administrators, it is important that you take vacations. I remember telling my board that I needed to take time off for self-care. I shared with them that I could not work at an optimal level unless I took time off. I was not requesting additional time. This time was time earned that due to the deadlines and other variables, I had not taken.

In another instance I shared with the Board that I would be unable to meet their expectations being one person. Needless to say, I did not last long after that. I had to transition out for my personal health and well-being, both physically and mentally. Because of this experience, I've always ensured that my team took vacation. In fact, at times, I would prompt managers to ensure staff took vacation time. I did not want them to lose their time. I also wanted them to have the balanced life that I did not. Functioning in dysfunction.

As a parent nurtures a child, we nurture our team. We must care for them and tend to their needs regardless of how awful they may have treated us. Regardless of their performance on the job. There may be a reason that we are unaware of that is causing this behavior. We must show compassion to our team just as we show compassion to our consumers. If they witness you leading by example, it can become easier to cross train and they will witness your compassion in action. I often shared with my team that I have done their job before and understand the challenges and work it entails. This was more important to them than my open door policy. I was not just a pencil pusher but one who cared.

Within this place of dysfunction, we must remember that no matter how stressed and frustrated we become, our role at times, is to assume many other roles in order to keep the cultural morale high. It is our role to establish the normal or new normal. The new normal can be identified as the changes you make to the organizational structure and culture during your tenure. There may be resistance but the new normal is necessary in order to move forward. For this reason, we tolerate behaviors that would otherwise be unacceptable in other places. At times we overcompensate for what the team has not received, such as a cost of living increase or merit awards. We become more tolerable of poor behavior and function within this dysfunction.

In time, these behaviors are remedied through the implementation of human resource policies and procedures that are updated annually and are aligned with the State and Federal labor laws.

It is noteworthy to mention the purpose for an Employee Manual is to protect both the employer and employee.

Again, this may not be your story, but they are my experiences and I know I am not alone in this dysfunctional culture of nonprofit.

"We are often told to never burn bridges, but sometimes we need to burn the bridge to make sure we never cross it again."

FRIENDS AND FOES

In the nonprofit culture, there are those with whom we work closely and appear to be friends of our mission, vision and passion. The two leaders work well together, support each others' work and listen to the woes of the nonprofit challenges. Then, there are those who want nothing more than to see you fail and the agency close. I have experienced both of these throughout my years in nonprofit.

Understand that there will always be people who do not like your mere existence. They know nothing about you but you are breathing and it bothers them. No matter how cordial you treat them, no matter how kind or accommodating you are to them, they will never accept you or your role as an administrator. These people, I thought were consummate professionals and supportive until I learned they had a mission to remove me from my position. Not because they desired the role, they wanted to run things like organized crime. There were those with whom they conspired who too had rankings within the "cartel". They would bully staff by threatening to physically fight or use their position of leadership to intimidate and control the environment. This was like nothing I had ever seen before.

These individuals wrote anonymous letters to the Board of Directors making all sorts of false accusations and attacking my character. At the time I was not aware of any of these things going on because I was focused on getting my work done and ensuring the staff was not bullied by these people; fearful of losing their jobs. They wanted me OUT! I thought they were friends but they were really foes. During this course I would receive anonymous letters and emails. Complaints came to the agency from the Equal Employment Opportunity Commission laced with false accusations. They attempted every means to get rid of me. They even contacted funders telling them they would not go away silently and even threatened lawsuits. I was only made aware of these anonymous letters sent to the Board after time had passed. These people became a fiery force against me. Had no one known my history or my character, this group of people could have destroyed my career with their character assassination.

Because of my work ethic, I kept my head held high and continued to move forward with the work of the mission. Remember, you must be married to the mission, so there is no time to separate during difficult times. You must remain committed even though it looks as though you have no support from your leadership. Continue to persevere because in the end the consumers need the services that are provided by the organization you serve.

These are the dysfunctions that we continue to function in because we do not want to breach confidentiality of the agency. You want to maintain the reputation of the organization and its governing board of well respected individuals. It gets addressed one time during a meeting never to be discussed again. It is during those times where you hear from your colleagues that your job is being offered by a foe who in person appears to be a friend. "Functioning in the dysfunction". Is this normal behavior to ignore what we see as dysfunctions within an organization? While inside, how do we deal with the breaches within the infrastructure? We are expected to perform regardless of any situation or circumstance. We work feverishly to strategize on how to document our outcomes, increase our funding and strategize with no help from the board who reminds us that they are in fact volunteers.

Understand that often times within the nonprofit sector, we are vying for the same funds, serving many of the same consumers and facing the same challenges within our organizational structures be it with friends or foes.

***

How do we differentiate our Friends from Foes within this culture? In my 20 plus years serving the nonprofit community, I have met many people who I've seen scale the walls to leadership. Their leadership roles have been from within, through serving the same community, or through transitioning from one agency to another. Within the context of nonprofits in the Urban setting, at minimum the life of healthy leadership expands between fifteen to twenty-five years. I began my work in nonprofit as an Administrative Assistant and many of the colleagues I have today I met during our time working for various agencies and programs. These are the people I call upon when I need a source, shoulder and often times hope. These people, true friends in the work, are invaluable and will remain faithful and close throughout the years. My suggestion, is when you meet friends who remain true and not those who are fair weather and will not betray your trust, hold on to them. They will walk you through the toughest times in your career.

These friends are those close collaborators and partners who provide letters of support for our proposals. These friends are those who you congratulate when you both are awarded funding from the same source. These friends are the ones who you can call on when you have that one family you are compelled to assist and your award has been spent. Can you assist this family? Do you have any shelter beds available? Do you have room for one more? The answer is yes, eight out of ten times. These are the relationships that are reciprocal. This is the cultivating culture of partnerships and collaborations, especially within the social service sector. These partnerships are never one sided. We keep in mind that we are married to our missions and its benefactors the consumers. To these partners we never have to extend the olive branch because it is always available.

Along the way, competition can set in, but don't lose sight of the mission and vision of your agency. You see, these are the matters that no one addresses. In the struggle of this work, we need people around us who can relate to our woes when we are awaiting payment from a reimbursable grant for which we've provided services. When the Board of Directors don't understand the challenges we face and are more interested in governing then ensuring we are connected to the right people, working on behalf of the agency by supporting through their time, talents and treasures. We need sounding boards who cannot be those whom we lead.

There are lots of books that speak to the challenges of managing nonprofits but this is the time to discuss the practical challenges of the nonprofit culture. It's time to be transparent and speak out about the backbiting culture that exists within a compassionate environment. Yes, this is an oxymoron. That is why we are "functioning in dysfunction".

We are often told to never burn bridges, but sometimes we need to burn the bridge to make sure we never cross it again.

"Ensure your church and CDC staff do not overlap in roles and responsibilities because this presents a conflict of interest."

FAITH-BASED ORGANIZATIONS

For those working within the faith-based community, you are met with varying challenges that may present themselves like those previously discussed. However, you must lean on your faith and adopt the mindset that the church and its Community Development Corporation (CDC) are a business. You must secure professionals who are trained and skilled for the work of the mission. It is not best practice to hire members of the congregation to oversee all matters of the CDC. Your Board of Directors should not be comprised of church members and/or friends only. It should be reflective of the targeted community served. Your Board members should be those who possess skills, knowledge and resources that will aid in moving the organization's mission and vision forward.

Although there are well meaning individuals who volunteer to provide services, it is important that you hire someone to manage the finances of the CDC or secure a reliable volunteer who is business minded with a finance background.

Ensure your church and CDC staff do not overlap in roles and responsibilities because this presents a conflict of interest. To prevent such conflicts, employ the practice of separating business of the church from business of the CDC. In fact, neither should there be a co-mingling of funds.

I worked with a faith-based organization that was not aware that their nonprofit status had been revoked because they had neglected to file their 990 tax reporting for three consecutive years. A very well meaning volunteer was responsible for this task and because no one was checking on this person to follow up on the tax filings, it was overlooked and their status was revoked. There was trust and no accountability. In fact, the Pastor was unaware that the status had been revoked. However, when it was brought to his attention the matter was rectified and the nonprofit status was reinstated.

A well operated faith-based organization has all of its checks and balances aligned and is operating at an optimal level. These checks and balances include, but are not limited to, employing best practices by eliminating conflicts of interest, subscribe to current employment laws and provide manuals for programs and general operations. When addressing ethical concerns, relating to the general operation of the day-to-day functions, there are written guidelines to adhere to. Although you are faith-based you should operate in an efficient manner and ascribe to basic business acumens.

This work is also grueling and met with overworked and burned out volunteers and staffers. The previous contents in this book also apply to you and your work. You should never make the assumption that because someone is within the community of faith that they do not have ulterior motives and are necessarily aligned with the mission and vision of the CDC. Keep your eyes open for the abuse of power and have systems set in place to prevent such things from perpetuating itself resulting in people abandoning the cause and mission. Although faith-based, you are a nonprofit organization and should adhere and take note of how to navigate the dysfunctions within nonprofit management.

Further, within the faith-based context, I suggest you be careful when placing a clergy person under the supervision of a lay person. This makes for an unhealthy environment if all persons do not possess spiritual maturity. The lay person, if not mature, may feel they have full spiritual authority over the clergy person. Again, this may work if there is a mature lay person who can differentiate the roles, but in some cases this makes for a very strained work environment. However, the greater danger lies when there is an employed clergy person who is seminary trained and reports to someone who does not possess business acumens but was able to manipulate themselves into a position of authority.

Make the investment to secure professionals that will guide and move the mission of your CDC and do not use someone who says they can do it but rather someone who has the expertise and a successful track record. It is also important that as an organization, you have in place an Employee Procedure Manual, Board Manual, job descriptions, Fiscal Policy Manual and a General Operations Manual. These items outline the expectations and requirements in place to keep everyone accountable. These items and additional Program Manuals are staples within community-based nonprofit organizations. If you are a Community-Based organization and do not have these manuals or other documents, I suggest you begin to put these systems in place. I have found that when these documents are present, staff are better equipped to carry out their job functions and meet the expectations of the organization.

"I've never been empowered by watching others. I became empowered when I gained the confidence to believe in my own potential."

SURVIVAL: HOW TO STAY AFLOAT

We've discussed many of the dysfunctions that we navigate on a regular basis. The golden question is "How do I stay afloat?" How do you function when the board is more interested in governing than in partnering? How do you not drown in the mundane tasks of the day, week, month and vision for the year? How do you not become the type of person and/or leader that you always said you would never be? There's only twenty-four hours in the day and eight to twelve hours in the normal social service nonprofit work day. How do I not drown in development, work plans, communication plans, staff development planning, assessing the work of the agency, capturing measurable outcomes and impact of the work you are contracted to perform? How? How do you continue to serve an organization of which you are passionate about the work and mission while becoming stressed out about the actual performance of the work? How do you stay afloat while ensuring that every program meets its contracted level of service? How do you stay afloat when the need for funding overshadows the mission and vision of the organization?

These are the questions nonprofit leaders juggle on a regular basis. How do we not get taken under by wave after wave? The tide gets high and we continue to swim. Where is your life jacket? Is there anyone throwing out the lifeline? Are you able to signal an S.O.S when you're in distress? Can you believe these thoughts are continually swarming through our brains to the point we awaken each day with a series of these questions and begin strategizing on how we will actually navigate throughout the day, while also putting out staffing fires?

As I was writing this, I thought how could I have ever survived this and lived to tell the story! I was able to get out and write about my encounters to help others in this same situation and let them know that what they are experiencing is not far fetched. You are not alone in your functioning within a dysfunctional system. There are so many others who do not dare speak of the challenges in fear of being under-minded by peers. I thought a colleague wanted to work with me and was excited about the opportunity when I learned that his only interest was in his personal gain. Once the person received everything he needed from me, he began to exclude me from the conversations and the work. I remember sharing my strategy and approach with a Board member. I told him what my approach would be in order to push a certain agenda in order to more effectively move the organization. As we sat in the meeting and I began to make my recommendations, this individual threw a monkey wrench into the plan that others would have agreed to, had he not spoken against my plan.

In another instance I had someone offer my job to a colleague who in turn told me about the offer. It was not only offered by someone who had nothing to do with the agency I served at the time, it was witnessed by eight other colleagues who were upset that this conversation was happening.   I know it's hard to believe but I stayed afloat.

***

Swimming is the active movement to and from another location mentally or physically. In the previous chapters you are swimming. There is movement. You are making movements in various directions. You are navigating the waters. You even change techniques at times. Sometimes you need to change positions in order to see clearly and adapt to the environment in an effort to determine its navigation and move accordingly. Remember, you are not wearing a life jacket so if you completely stop and give up, you will drown. Keep moving.

When on an airplane and waiting for the flight to take off, the airline steward instructs passengers what to do in the event that the airplane Is In trouble and the oxygen mask drops. They say, "first place the mask over your face before assisting anyone else". Well, in this instance, we cannot keep anyone else afloat if we do not wear our life jacket that will keep us afloat. However, if we attempt to assist others without first putting on our life jacket, we will use the basic technique learned for beginning swimmers; the doggie paddle! As long as you paddle you continue to move and stay afloat.

What happens when you can no longer paddle? You change position. You lay on your back and float or you swim. However, there are times in which you need to sit back, rest and regroup. This is when you lay on your back and float. Floating is taking time off to clear your mind and restore balance to your life. Floating is taking a mental health day every now and then. Floating is setting your alarm to ensure you leave the office at a reasonable hour. Floating is restoring balance between your professional and personal life.

My advice to you is don't wait for affirmations. You must learn to be your loudest cheerleader! Believe in yourself, celebrate your successes and learn and grow from your failures.

The key to staying afloat determines how you perceive yourself. I've never been empowered by watching others. I became empowered when I gained the confidence to believe in my own potential.

SHIFTING WITH THE TIDE

There comes a time when things quiet down. The waters begin to recede and the tide shifts. Now you can stand up because the water is only to your waste. There is no need to paddle or float. Use this time of calm to recalibrate. This is when you have more time to sit and readjust your operational systems. What are your Board tenures? Are there any? Can members serve in perpetuity? This can be a great challenge especially during times when a shifting in the mission and culture of the organization is needed. You'll need fresh ideas, innovative thinking and new resources.

Is there a need for an Advisory Board, where workers are needed? An Advisory Board who will volunteer with an expectation to serve and not sit idle with a critical view of the organization and does not come to the defense of the staff for fear of being rejected by their peers. Do you have a Board who reminds you monthly that they are volunteers and do not assist in any way? In fact, they do not have a required annual donation. You send constant reminders and even mention it at meetings with no response to the request.

I believe every Board should have a "give or get" requirement in their by-laws. They either "give" a required amount from their personal resources or they "get" the required amount through personal contacts. This would be a shift in the tide.

Take time to craft the proper language and garner support from the majority of the board, seal it with an amendment to the by-laws and you now have a requirement for your Board members and an increase to your budget donations.

It is also during this time where you can form a committee of staff and Board members to plan a fundraiser that will be an annual event that will yield a considerable amount of resources to support general operating expenses that are not covered within any grant. This will be one major fundraiser while there can also be additional smaller fund-raisers throughout the year.

Your best planning is done when the tide shifts. Work Plan. Check. Development Plan. Check. Communications Plan. Check. Staff Evaluations. Check.

During these times you re-calibrate to focus on matters that determine the sustainability of your organization. This is the time to determine if and when to outsource services that will decrease staffing expenses. You have more time to focus on administrative tasks when the tide shifts. There is no danger because you're not wearing a life jacket. You can stand firm and don't have to worry about drowning in the abyss of the water that is trying to consume you. There is no extra energy to exert because you can stand without thinking about a device to keep you afloat.

This is the time to make changes. During this time, your decisions are more rational and not reactive due to a situation that arose. During this time your critical thinking skills are heightened. This is the time to re-establish structure and order that may have presented problems in the past.

I recommend all annual staff performance evaluations be conducted the same time each year. This is manageable for a staff of fifty or less. This system has proven to be more efficient than attempting to manage start dates of each staff member because they all differ. For new hires, the first thirty to sixty-days of employment should be your standard practice for performance evaluations. The next evaluation will then be during the annual performance review month.

The month you select for annual performance evaluations should not be a busy month for the organization. Select a slow period to ensure no staff member is omitted due to the workload of their supervisor, who is responsible for conducting such reviews.

In the long run, this strategy and other systems can save you a lot of time and energy.

"A team member does what is required. A team player get's in the game and assists wherever needed."

DISMANTLING AND RECONSTRUCTING A DYSFUNCTIONAL CULTURE

We've addressed what dysfunction looks like. It's character, nature, behaviors, mindset and sense of entitlement to what one believes belongs to or is due them. We've addressed the many behaviors that come to the surface when people feel entitled and things are not going their way. We've even looked at things from a culture of social service nonprofit organizations where "colleagues" at times, are not friends. They are foes who mask their friendships very well until your gut instincts reveal the signs to you and reveal their true intent.

Within the social service nonprofit there are distinctions due to the nature of the work, level of stress factors, governance and community relations and engagement that is involved in carrying out the work of the mission.

In order to survive and change the internal systems, in an effort to shift the culture of functioning within this dysfunctional system, there needs to be a dismantling and reconstruction. Let's look at the approach I took in dismantling a dysfunctional culture.

At the heart of the work being done through social services and in most human service nonprofit organizations is the passion of the employee or team member, which I referred to those who were under my supervision. People should be treated with dignity and respect. This for me, was and remains paramount. If people do not feel as though they matter and have no voice in their day-to-day job tasks, they are not invested in the work they do and cannot fully grasp the mission of the organization. When one does not grasp the mission or vision it effects their morale and they then are merely working for a paycheck.

It is important to be a leader who is compassionate about your team. It is important to understand the personal needs of your team, without becoming too personal or cross boundaries. As a leader it is important that your team knows with confidence that you support them in their work. It is important that you lead from the front and not behind. It is important for you to lead by example. A leader should not be too high and mighty that they cannot assist their team whenever possible. If the telephones are ringing...answer them. By them hearing you engage, it teaches them not only on how to answer the phones properly but how to engage difficult consumers. When your team sees you coming outside of your job description to assist, they too will transition from team members to team players. A team member does what is required. A team player get's in the game and assists wherever needed.

Your first step in dismantling is to break down all of the factors that contribute to low and poor team morale. Give your team a voice. Ask what they think would be best to perform their daily tasks. They have great contributions to their work, especially given the fact that they are performing these tasks on a daily basis. It is important that the team understands that they are an asset and that they have a voice that is being heard. They need to know that their contribution is not only welcomed but is respected and will be included in the procedures for their role in the organization. When the team member sees their recommendations being implemented it chips away at the dysfunction and the dismantling begins.

I suggest you employ staff building activities and events such as staff appreciation day where you acknowledge the efforts of the entire team. Host a friends and family day for staff and their families. Before a busy holiday season plan something for the staff to enjoy and partake in before the busy holiday rush. When working for a particular organization, we knew the holiday season would call for extra long hours and a busy schedule, to say the least. We would provide toys, clothing and turkeys for well over five thousand families during the course of the holiday season. As a result, leadership would give us the entire week off with pay after Christmas. This is how they showed their appreciation for the team.

So often there is dismantling without reconstruction. It is not a good practice to dismantle a system without having a new and improved system in place. If the old program or employee manuals are not longer useful, they must be revised to fit the new structure and culture of the organization. It is important to reconstruct the methods of communicating with team members. A former colleague introduced me to the sandwich method for times you need to communicate poor performance to a team member. The method is that you begin and end with positive words and in the middle you give the hard message. This is especially useful when needing to address job performance. The old method would be to address the issue right away with soft words. I have learned throughout my career that no matter how much sugar you use to coat a negative message the impact is the same without a positive word. If we are completely honest with ourselves, we would admit that it is easier to take a negative criticism if we hear something positive about what we are doing or have done. I have come to learn that you get more flies with honey than you do with vinegar. It is also important to realize that when dismantling you are interrupting the current culture of the organization.

The dismantling and reconstruction process requires change and change is not easy for everyone. In fact, you should expect push back when you begin to dismantle and while you are reconstructing. During this process constant communication and engagement with your team is key. Dismantling and reconstruction do not happen overnight but with gradual shifts the transformation process is smoother.

It is during the reconstruction phase when you must invest in your staff. How can you motivate and encourage a consumer/client and not your team? In fact, the greatest investment you can make as a nonprofit leader is in developing your team. Understand you are not investing in their future at your agency, you are investing in them as a whole person for them to thrive wherever they may land in their career.

"In order to stay afloat while navigating the dysfunctions within nonprofit management, you must ride the wave."

CONCLUSION

You are here. We are here. Know that on this journey you are not alone. Know that you have the strength to navigate these waters. Understand your strengths and weaknesses. You should never dull your brilliance for anyone! You should never "dummy down" your intellect to make someone feel better about themselves. Stop coming to the table empty handed but learn to navigate and drive the conversation. Understand that someone who supervises is not authorized to lord over you unless you permit it. Be courageous. Be the captain of your own ship, make career moves on your own terms and not based on the expectations of those around you. Write your own narrative! Face each day with a plan and an understanding that there will be roadblocks within each day. Embrace the new learning opportunities that present themselves before you.

In order to stay afloat while navigating the dysfunctions within nonprofit management, you must ride the wave. Ride the waves of every obstacle, every success and every failure. Ride the wave when your staff decides to veer left while you're guiding them to the right. Ride the wave when the Board does not respect your leadership and wants a face without a voice. Ride the wave when funding gets cut. Ride the wave when people within the community feel the organization you lead is no longer relevant. It is not personal. Ride the wave!!!

The tide will subside at times and you can paddle without trepidation of the waters. Then there are times when the waves appear to engulf you and water is flooding in your mouth, the winds are strong and you feel as though you are about to drown. Gain your balance and ride the wave to stay afloat! You have a greater balance than you know. Understand your strength is being built and your knowledge is being expanded. Learn, grow and ride the wave!

Remember that you are on your own terms and when it gets too much to bear and your family becomes a casualty, get out of the water. Know when enough is enough! While navigating this system you are also building your courage to survive; courage to take a leap of faith and courage to walk away when the time is right.

Mahatma Ghandi said, "Be the change you want to see in the world". It's up to you to determine where that change will occur. Ask yourself the question, "How will I show up"?

TESTIMONIALS

These are a few comments about my performance and professionalism sent to me from colleagues and clients.

- *"It was my pleasure to work with you through these years. You have shown passion, class and professionalism at all times. Your organization has grown by leaps and bounds under your tenure, and even though you are leaving I know the agency will continue the good work you've done there. I wish you well in whatever your next endeavor finds you doing and if you ever need anything you know how to reach me. Safe travels."*

- *"As is expected excellence follows your every gesture. THANK YOU!!"*

- *"I have my first paid client, thank you for your support*

- *"I did an entire separate video for you but lost it. I was saying to you how a part in your book reminded me of the importance of a mental health break"*

CONTACT:

Tonya R. Bryan

WWW.TONYABRYAN.COM

WWW.PNEUMACONSULTANTS.COM

www.ingramcontent.com/pod-product-compliance
Lightning Source LLC
Chambersburg PA
CBHW071256170526
45165CB00003B/1376